Limits of Control

Steve Spence lives in Plymouth and co-organises live poetry group The Language Club. His reviews and poetry have appeared in *Great Works, Shearsman, Stride, Tears in the Fence, Tenth Muse* and *The Rialto*. He was assistant editor of *Terrible Work* magazine for four issues and in 2007 completed an MA in Creative Writing at the University of Plymouth. His debut book, *A Curious Shipwreck* (Shearsman, 2010), was shortlisted for the Forward Prize for Best First Collection.

Limits of Control

Steve Spence

Penned in the Margins
LONDON

PUBLISHED BY PENNED IN THE MARGINS
22 Toynbee Studios, 28 Commercial Street, London E1 6AB
www.pennedinthemargins.co.uk

All rights reserved
© Steve Spence 2011

The right of Steve Spence to be identified as the author of this work has been asserted by him in accordance with Section 77 of the Copyright, Designs and Patent Act 1988.

This book is in copyright. Subject to statutory exception and to provisions of relevant collective licensing agreements, no reproduction of any part may take place without the written permission of Penned in the Margins.

First published 2011

ISBN
978-0-9565467-8-4

This book is sold subject to the condition that it shall not, by way of trade or otherwise, be lent, re-sold, hired out, or otherwise circulated without the publisher's prior consent in any form of binding or cover other than that in which it is published and without a similar condition including this condition being imposed on the subsequent purchaser.

Acknowledgements

Some of these poems have previously appeared in the following magazines and websites: *Shadowtrain*, *Stride*, *Tears in the Fence*.

Many thanks are due to Anthony Caleshu and Tony Lopez for encouraging me to undertake the MA in Creative Writing at the University of Plymouth. Thanks are also due to members of The Language Club who have provided feedback, encouragement and friendship over a long period, particularly Tim Allen, Norman Jope, Kenny Knight and Philip Kuhn. I'm also indebted to Damaris Barber for friendship, feedback and encouragement without which I may well have given up.

Contents

Voices of the dead	15
Memoirs of a tour manager	16
Every cloud has its day	17
The function of lying	18
Are you an all-round polymath	19
Gardens are a source of fascination	20
Is there a viper in the nest?	21
Bracing doesn't begin to describe it	22
Today we're going to look for pyramids	23
This remains a place of broken dreams	24
Does your English let you down?	25
She's not there	26
Explanatory notes	27
Malice in Wonderland	28
Shipwreck butter	29
Mystery attracts mystery	30
Training is provided	31
Such is the importance of shipwrecks	32
It's an idea that promotes hostility	33
How did the compound eye evolve?	34
The truth must be told	35
Are you a risk-taker?	36
Uses and abuses of a musical icon	37
King Kong	38
The architecture of despair	39
It pays to treat the polls with caution	40
Fresh raw fish straight from the sea	41

Star gazing	42
"Do you miss the dance of politics?"	43
The longest day will soon begin	44
Dark secrets of the universe	45
Do you want to earn and learn?	46
Breaking news	47
Austerity rules, okay!	48
The struggle ahead will be fierce	49
It was like stepping into the abyss	50
The language of clouds	51
Your proposal may have merit	52
Chinese gold consumption may double	53
Tomorrow, the real debate begins	54
Fear, anxiety and indecision	55
Is this a kangaroo court?	56
The voices of doubt	57
Health and safety	58
More snow is on the way	59
The word cloud	60
The empire builder	61
Wild beasts	62
That's the way to do it	63
The girl with the pirate tattoo	64
In search of big fish	65
Without sponsors there is no expedition	66
Living in the past	67
The gathering storm	68
The gravy train	69
The American Dream	70
Morning glory	71

How to spot a swallow   72
Their lofty aims   73
The surveillance state   74
Meltdown   75
Transgression and taboo   76

for Susie Hatch

Limits of Control

Voices of the dead

Knowing how to feel is more important than what you feel. This surely depends less on the robots than on the quality of the humans who design them. Should beauty be painted with her head in the clouds? She still has occasional mood swings but they're nowhere near as severe. From the water everything looks different yet most learning happens casually and without programmed instruction. A system of uncertainty has entered our daily lives. Pollack like a slow-moving bait and for that reason the action of your rubber eel is important. As mutinies go this is a very laid-back affair. Some scientists say that our planet is running out of platinum. This may or may not be true but every cloud has its moment in the sun. During the manic phase there can be feelings of inflated self-esteem verging on grandiosity. Do you have the ability to spot the next big thing?

Memoirs of a tour manager

Give me a vision of the future. Once again it is the rod that does most of the work. A new, or at least more confident, do-it-yourself politics flourished out of necessity. Have you ever come across a storm-surge? Purnell Roberts is dead. It's difficult to control or anticipate what a robot might learn on the battlefield. Yet schooling is imposed on all citizens for between ten and eighteen years. As an actor he wished always to be detached from the part he was playing. Are you a wild swimmer? Everything swirled about him like a cloud yet people with mild mania are often witty and inventive. Was the war legal or not? All candidates are required to complete section 2B of the application form. When there is a crisis we will deal with the crisis. It could be said that we all employ some form of camouflage yet astronomers are waking up to brilliant, celestial views. Like all small children he was fascinated by the typewriter.

Every cloud has its day

Do you still enjoy swimming in neglected places? What we mean by freedom is not always clear yet somebody needs to pick up a gauntlet and run with it. It's good to be in a museum after dark. The writing on the wall remains an interesting thing for us to look at yet it was fishing that cemented his love of the natural world. A hooked mullet is an entirely different proposition. Johnny Dankworth has died. It may take another crisis to prompt radical reform yet wasps thrive mainly when there is a fine spring and a mild summer. The most dangerous shark is the one you don't see. That is all I can remember about teaching myself to read yet there is a fine line between telling the truth and telling a lie. A wreck is like a reef that falls from out of the sky. Do you think he plans it all out or makes it up as he goes along? Yes, but are we talking about real emotion or counterfeit feelings?

The function of lying

Soon the turbulence became much more severe. Whale sharks are exciting because of their sheer size but if you go for a brain scan you have to keep very still. In the event, a major organisation has been established, bringing together all kinds of local groups and individuals. There's a popular myth that flirting with chaos is something we all grow out of. Has the wasp an important role in our eco-system? This is the question on every cloud-spotter's lips. Moonlight drains everything of substance yet how can we be sure that the gold we wear is as pure as it looks? The immediate effect of this was to lessen his anxiety and to allow him to appear normal. In choosing whether or not to lie we generally weigh benefits against potential harm. An interest in mature women comes later, with experience. Do you see total nudity as a path to freedom? With age everything starts to remind you of something else.

Are you an all-round polymath?

Please tell us about yourself. What skills, experience and qualities can you bring to this position? Dark clouds are gathering over this secretive and quirky place. Are you considering a moonlight flit? This question was as interesting to the class as it had always been to me. I don't know about therapy but we were definitely on the financially illiterate spectrum. Yet we just lay there listening to the clouds. Is mental time-travel unique to humans? On the other hand, people who keep their resolutions tend to break their goals into smaller steps. One must troll very slowly to catch Pollack yet the numeracy of the Egyptians was widely admired across the ancient world. There are no polar bears but there are killer whales and seals instead. When threatened they present their unappetising disguise to the intruder. If the strike is delayed too long the fish may drop the bait altogether.

Gardens are a source of fascination

Most notable of all has been the support from marginalized and oppressed groups. Have you ever come across a goldfinch? It strikes me that both clouds and governments are instruments of seduction yet what are men compared to rocks and mountains? Making papyrus is a laborious process but it's also quite straightforward and the end result provides a wonderful surface to write on. The core problem is that we have lost our respect for food. During the recession more and more people have been trading in their old gold. Application packs and further information can be downloaded from our website. Where do the bumblebees in my garden actually come from? Twelve hours later the intruders left the ship and allowed it to continue on its passage. Wildlife is never predictable and opening your moth trap is like opening a birthday present. Why not consider the seamy side of charity?

Is there a viper in the nest?

Once extinguished, a city's soul can't just be conveniently revived. Is criticism of the bankers an affirmation? For all their mystical language the Ranters expressed a wonderful sense of exuberant reverence and earthly nonconformity. If the mullet wants to run you should let it run. Both parties emphasised the importance of the small farmer and we'll be hearing from both sides involved in this clandestine conflict. Today we have a tireless capacity for sustained concentration. Not only was there no ship but the rain came down in buckets and we had no shelter. If this is a criminal act it seems to be following a new business model. Good design should stand the test of time yet we looked around to make sure that nobody was watching. Now people are seeing piracy in its true colours after a long history of Hollywood romance. When fishing from a height a drop net is essential.

Bracing doesn't begin to describe it

Nervous truth-tellers often exhibit the same anxieties as liars yet depression is becoming as big a problem as heart disease. His musical skills were so poor that whenever he started to play she ran out of the room in a fit of hysterical laughter. Listening to him talk about the crisis you'd think the whole thing had happened to somebody else. Outdoor swimming can make you feel more alive. It turned out that the entire system had been built on sand so I put her in contact with someone with a passion for dance and ballet. Of all the common clouds, Cirrus must be the most beautiful. Weirpools are always popular places for swimming so what exactly took you to the Caribbean? Experience teaches us not to assume that the obvious is clearly understood yet any cloud becomes more beautiful in the light of dawn or dusk. Today, I have eaten my last eel.

Today we're going to look for pyramids

Let me be more precise – overhead there was a high bank of clouds. Appeals take weeks and even months to hear yet one is not going to learn to swim unless one gets into the water. Are you in favour of the evidence for global warming? There has been nothing like this economic catastrophe in the lives of working people for as long as we can recall. His hair was too long, his collar too large, his trousers too short and his shoes too big. Have you experienced the mysterious world of the magic mushroom? Let us learn always to expect the unexpected. Having delivered its message the cloud will be free to drift off and enjoy the splendour of the rainy season. His upbringing may have been bohemian but it wasn't sociable. Yes, but can you really compute the flood levels of the Nile? Those mullet look lazy and indolent, as if they have nothing to do and all day in which to do it.

This remains a place of broken dreams

He made his way through dark, deserted streets and climbed towards the sky. Beneath my outward calm I was slightly nervous yet what an effort it is to write this all down. Are the banks still keeping a gun to our heads? Global climate change is like a disaster in slow-motion. We are now a country ruled by fear yet early in the season the familiar rubber eel is the most successful lure. Do you possess a sound commercial instinct? Once the self-taught man or woman has been discredited, all non-professional activity is rendered suspect. This crisis was predictable yet I was unable to leave my hiding place until evening. Such a perverse redistribution of income from poor to rich is unprecedented in human history. All the time she stood like a statue and I could hear him breathing heavily. Don't get too intimate with a cloud.

Does your English let you down?

Many of the powers ascribed to the scent of vanilla can be traced to the link between memory and smell. I was unable to leave my hiding place until evening yet when the wind died down her worst fear became a reality. Yes, but is the alligator gar a natural born killer? She suddenly began to look very intensely at various objects in the room. In many ways the left hand is unaware of what the right hand is doing yet her documentary continues to unfold like a thriller. For another thing, some of these methods are barely methods at all. Why do so few men write love letters? Clouds in general have a huge, if contradictory, effect on ground temperatures, yet once seen, a painting by Nash is not easily forgotten. What she wants to use as a weapon will rebound upon us all. Jellied eels look revolting but cooked any other way the flesh is firm, white and delicious! His landscapes offer a curious blend of ancient and modern but the alligator gar is taking the rap for the alligator. This cloud is not known for its spontaneity.

She's not there

"You were brilliant. Great reading and good talk in between. Much better than Nancy. You should do the show." This happens in Spring and is characterised by hypo-mania and sexual adventurism. It is related to rising sap. Yet we are all obsessed by time and how little we have of it. Few sufferers of eating disorders blame their illness on pictures of skinny models yet he has organised the exhibition in a somewhat eccentric fashion. Nash's paintings are both timeless and of their time but I still want to find out if this creature has committed the crimes it's been accused of. Chaotic to their misty core, they do their best to confound our attempts at classification. Yet the strain of such decisions is enormous and can be felt for years to come. Some people absorb their good fortune and go on with their lives unaffected but we rarely, if ever, hear from them. "Films? When I expire maybe they will say of me – bury the fucker, he's dead!" Each of us builds, inside our head, a model of the world in which we find ourselves. Yet the strain of such decisions is enormous and can be felt for years to come.

Explanatory notes

Long before the last person has spoken, a feeling of warmth and camaraderie pervades the room. Just changing your attitude can affect the world around you. In other words, the people who don't have access to a corporation to which they can offer lifelong loyalty are the majority. After she got home she knew she was in dangerous territory. Yes, but all manner of people inhabit all manner of drinking houses. Here I shall sketch only the salient highlights in a formless, rambling way. Hurry up, please, it's time! By remaining a victim she has clearly become more comfortable. Yet when the road dips again there are stretches of marshland that one instinctively dislikes. Do you want to wear the hair shirt of fiscal rectitude? Ox's Chariot, a gold model from the ancient Persian Empire, almost two and a half thousand years old. Call me a contrarian but this all seems a bit too tidy. Yet a reverence for the military co-exists uneasily with an increasing scepticism about war. At the stroke of midnight the atmosphere suddenly changed. Billy Jenkins is back.

Malice in Wonderland

Physically she is present but her gaze seems to look into the past. "It's great to have a river running through a city." Rainbows may be the most familiar of the sky's optical delights but how many of us notice the finer points of their appearance? Outside we've joined sixty or so workers just starting the early shift. None of the audience made any move to leave yet looking at clothes is a key part of looking at history. We know the sea is big but its very vastness is seldom comprehended fully. Why continue to feel pain, paralysis and depression? Bright sunshine and bitter cold weather were the constants yesterday while the far South is due for rain, sleet and snow. It's been argued that the motive of human society is always, in the last resort, an economic one. More important, though, is the frame of mind you are in when cloud-spotting. Only beings who can reflect upon the fact that they are determined are capable of freeing themselves. Yes, but does winter make us miserable? How does a Cumulus humilis manage to grow and build?

Shipwreck butter

Here is a pile of things that people have put their work, talents and hopes into and it has come to nothing. On a crowded table candles and glasses can be a hazard. A chance encounter in a bookshop may change your life forever yet this year we need something altogether more robust. *Cold, crisp,/bright-eyed day./Vernacular modernity/ on my way – a/new 4 story/tower now/expected. Blue/doors saying/keep clear. Ciao, Phil.* All those patchworks of mohair, tartan, goat hair, vintage lace and ethnic embroidery. Her golden limbs were somewhat off-trend but she carried off her one-shoulder white Roman dress like a pro. Although his actions were quiet and rational he had a furtive, hunted look which his mother did not like. His lonely paintings are deliberately artificial yet the mood is exultant and awe-inspiring. We remain committed to reaching a resolution.

Mystery attracts mystery

For many artists the economic underpinning of their
career must be teaching. Yet we cater for everybody's needs,
whether novice or elite, with a wide range of swimwear.
Yes, but do you have an interest in UFOs and the
paranormal? It may soon be evident that the school is
as marginal to education as the witch doctor is to public
health. One by one, disgraced bankers are hitting
the comeback trail. For many of their loyal consumers,
no price is too high to pay for these branded goods. Finally,
there needs to be proof. When it comes to what a work of
art is about, the primary point is always to locate where
its strength lies. The clouds in the sky were as white as ice
and they raced in thin crystals over the surface of the moon.
"Are we talking about John Wyndham here or are we
talking about Wyndham Lewis?"

Training is provided

At the beginning of the story he found himself in an eerie location. Minutes passed and nothing happened yet the drawings and paintings from that period suggest a deeply troubled adolescence. Not everyone takes drapery seriously but I wouldn't call it rubber-stamping by any means. Once the oil begins to wash ashore, damage could be sudden and widespread yet there's something elemental in the first sight of a pike. Most of the visual tropes in these titles appear in his later works. Also at risk are whales, dolphins and blue-fin tuna. Salt may divide opinion but exotic varieties are all the rage, while anyone interested in the democratic process could do worse than study the group decisions made by pigeons in mid-flight. Beside marine mammals and fish, marine reptiles are also threatened. With great relief he realised that he too was a mere appearance dreamt by another.

Such is the importance of shipwrecks

Once the oil begins to wash ashore, damage will be sudden and widespread. It's not the sex but the way it's been commodified that's the problem. Now is the time to take control of your career and gain the leading edge. This is not the way to come to power, with weapons in your hands. Much better to make your approach on all-fours, yet they had small heads and their brains were less than a third of the size of modern human brains. Today we're looking at the effect of volcanoes on our environment. In the hallway there is a mirror which faithfully duplicates all appearances, yet tall, silent horsemen patrol the roads. How do we know that bats and birds developed wings independently? Previous experience is not essential as training is provided.

It's an idea that promotes hostility

Suddenly a bulky white shape loomed up ahead of us and we flashed on the second torch. It's very useful to have eyes sensitive enough to see by moonlight if you happen to be an owl. Clearly I am not dead but it's as well that the world thinks otherwise. To focus sharply both near and far is a luxury you can live without yet there's no way of safely provoking a volcano and then controlling it. Let us turn back to Homer for a moment. There was something abnormal about the whole business yet they appear to have left within ten minutes of the last murder. Sunlight can be blotted out for days, weeks or even months. Talking of which, you might like to consider the beneficial qualities of clouds. There is more to laying down a rubby dubby trail than just hanging a bag over the side of the boat.

How did the compound eye evolve?

Is this the decade in which we stop worrying and learn to love modern art? I swung out onto the road and was about to reply when the phone rang. It's a long way from Greece to Britain but the garfish is a very fast and active fish. Here I shall sketch only the salient highlights in a formless, rambling way. Do you have a disability or a long-term health issue? Yet the invasion took part as planned and the country descended into chaos. On account of its narrow beak, or bill, it's a difficult fish to hook, yet we are focusing on the clean-up and not concerned with attributing blame. Despite the disastrous failings of intelligence, no one so far has apologised or been sacked. You will demonstrate competence in all aspects of office administration, including photocopying, filing, message-taking and collation. Here we are looking at a worst-case scenario.

The truth must be told

With the volcano still erupting the situation is continuously changing yet nobody seems to know why the bees are disappearing. If you stay still for long enough by the waterside things begin to happen. Make no mistake about it – this product is dangerous. Sheep have never seemed to me to be good companions for an insomniac but I've never done this before and it's a wonderfully absorbing task. Everywhere there are statues – hundreds of statues. Her room was an exercise in low-key chic, with crisp linens, a free-standing bath and a power-shower with more than the usual number of nozzles. When something becomes fetishized, capitalism steps in and finds a way of selling it. You should be firm but light-handed, keeping up a steady pressure all the time. Yes, but do you need to be rich to be green?

Are you a risk-taker?

A strong experience in the present awakens in the creative writer a memory of an earlier experience. By this time we were both a little drunk and I was reluctant for the evening to end. Far from exposing him to oblivion, this exposure brought him a genuine celebrity, yet the concept of plagiarism has ceased to exist. In each case, the facts have proved extremely difficult to establish. How did it come about that so preposterous a system was able to last for more than twenty minutes? She is exotic in the extreme, appearing like a bird of paradise in an otherwise neutral crowd. Yet *The Voodoo Wasps* are about to be recruited in the war on agricultural pests. Small wonder that our ancestors attributed these events to the moodiness of the gods. Take the first exit and ensure that you move into the far right-hand lane. The same is often true of biological materials.

Uses and abuses of a musical icon

Things cannot go on as if nothing has happened yet the events which follow are even more strange. If you don't feel like a submissive then a dominatrix won't make you behave like one. Yes, but aren't you curious to see who you might be matched with? Big retinas are always better than small retinas. Among my new friends is a beautiful redhead with Goth tendencies and a tart sense of humour. All our lenses include a scratch-resistant treatment at no extra charge. As their records attest, they didn't remain incompetent for all that long yet he virtually lived on the breadline and dedicated his life to charity. Secure behind their high walls and surveillance cameras, these estates constitute a chain of closed communities. Big retinas are always better than small retinas.

King Kong

Returning to the submarine he turned off the lights and sat thinking in the dark. How close to the oyster beds is the oil-spill now? Most jobs coming up soon are in the service sector yet monofilament line is not really suitable for this type of fishing. "My name is Roger. I have few interests but I am obsessed with mowing the lawn." These are far from easy colour combinations yet knitwear and casual tops are particularly popular this year. If things get out of hand, just remember that soda siphons work on much the same principle as fire extinguishers. This product is available in cream, red and black and is guaranteed to make a statement in any kitchen. Are they real people or are they real people pretending to be robots. Nowadays, speech synthesis can sound extremely natural indeed.

The architecture of despair

It was around this time that he began to write down scenes from his early childhood. This is a very plausible setting for a shipwreck. As an experimental auctioneer he should have been aware of the law yet microbes are probably the most diverse life forms on earth. As well as the rain there will be a cold wind making it quite miserable today. She continues to play the clarinet in her spare moments yet the purpose of this interview is to assess your suitability for the above post. However, small venues are better for sustaining that edgy quality in performance. As it turned out, the news was not as bad as analysts had predicted. When sprayed on a surface the glass solution forms a flexible, ultra-thin film, yet the map, while teeming with life, is actually all about death. This is a very plausible setting for a shipwreck.

It pays to treat the polls with caution

To try to predict the timing of the next economic downturn is ridiculous yet sinister forces are undeniably abroad in the world. It was a cowed sort of place, very gloomy and suffused with melancholy. The sublime truth of this fact entered me with such force that I had to gasp for breath. It's hard to believe this high temple of style has fallen into ruin yet on my way over to the bookshelf I noticed the sea chart. This living room is fantastic and has lots of light. Yes, but where do the map makers source their knowledge? Online competition is hardly a new phenomenon yet surely this is the great thing about circus training. Each of us is an eco-system, crawling with microbes. Right now we are emerging from a long winter's sleep into an uncertain future.

Fresh raw fish straight from the sea

Is improvisation at the heart of music therapy? All successful candidates will be vetted by the employer before taking up appointment. "Do you ever yearn to write a bodice-ripper?" There is no sleight of hand here yet chaos evidently provides us with a bridge between the laws of physics and the laws of chance. We thought we were changing the world but all we were doing was changing the look of the world. This slick, in all its different hues and consistencies, just goes on and on. The erotic charge of the paintings is surely why they are so good yet for all their shiny assurances none of them really knows what is going to happen. How much more of this oil can the ocean absorb?

Star gazing

He was a restless innovator, always looking for new ways to record the world. Yes, but how are your transferable skills? A rumour began to circulate that the fish was a halibut yet his colours are muted and tasteful, the brushwork delicate. Will the markets really give us the benefit of the doubt? It would be extremely useful if you could behave like a large Praying Mantis. This is a mess that is not going to go away. In the middle of an economic hurricane you don't usually give a weather forecast yet the scale of the slick is numbing. Language problems can often affect life or death decisions. His brushwork is lush and fluid yet he drinks too much and lives like a pig. It will be mainly cloudy today with scattered showers and a moderate N.E. wind.

"Do you miss the dance of politics?"

Life on the archipelago was notoriously bleak yet we covered everything from Hank Williams to Abstract Expressionism. By day she was a human resources manager but her passion was for heavy metal. When a promise has been made here there is no turning back. Do you want to swim in Homer's wine-dark sea? The main requirement is a clear flight path so that the bees are above head height and avoid flying into people. There was an ethos of experimentation and creativity which fed into the music yet it was clear that the army chiefs had been expecting a different outcome. "For goodness sake, why don't you just paint something that means something to you!" His death brought tributes from across the political spectrum.

The longest day will soon begin

All have been, or may shortly be, swept away by
the financial storm. We regard this theft as an act
of desecration. As always, it was a war for the
survival of democracy yet the gas is quite inert
and has no harmful effect on the environment.
The challenge was not to reproduce his voice but
to make the speech sound natural and smooth.
I had no choice but to break up the expedition
yet being part of a crowd doesn't diminish you,
it makes you stronger. We have contingency plans
for all eventualities. Yes, but how far away is the
oil? It's a misconception to think that bees won't
thrive in cities and towns although it's fair to say
this method has never been tried in deep water.

Dark secrets of the universe

It was a well-planned and co-ordinated attack yet translation, like politics, remains the art of the possible. When you are sure that the fish is ready then you should draw it towards the shore. This could turn out to be the biggest disaster for many decades yet it's a great day to be a particle physicist. Did you know that the Parthenon was originally a bank? This time it was my float that began to quiver. When the onion begins to brown, add the strained tomato pulp and leave to cool for five minutes, stirring all the time. A spokesman for the White House said it strongly condemned the violence. Such fantasies repel us or leave us cold yet a nameless scent was now curiously mixed with another scarcely less offensive odour.

Do you want to earn and learn?

Of all weather phenomena clouds are surely the most interesting. He grew vague when questioned about the details of battle yet his oratory is still recalled with awe today by those who were around to hear it. Sharp black jackets are teamed with retro-lace knickers and knee-length shorts. The scale of the problem means that green technology is unlikely to be enough. Clearly, our mission to persuade the world to look up and notice the clouds is far from over. Omnipotence may survive only in fairy tales, in childhood, in neurosis and in dreams yet death squads roam the streets with impunity. You must have a proven track record within a similar role.

Breaking news

Everything was done by hint and allusion yet a devotion to physical perfection had come to rule their lives. How has Britain changed in the fifteen years since the pirates came to power? Sometimes we use words in their most literal sense yet the idea of liberty is not incompatible with the existence of certain clouds. He was always opposed to violence although he was not an absolute pacifist and advocated an extreme form of direct action. For this position you will need to be organised and have a practical approach to administration. The influence of technology is scarcely a new story in fashion yet all animals have to deal with their world and the objects in it.

Austerity rules, okay!

I have been here too long but I have yet to find a suitable guide who can guess where I am going. Cash remains the most important method of payment for small transactions yet their manifesto promises to maintain current levels of defence spending. Successful applicants will be required to provide an enhanced disclosure. It is low tide and directly below the doorway the shore lies exposed. Fifteen miles off the coast a sea turtle is seen struggling through the slick. Coral reefs in many parts of the world now face devastation yet she is as trendily crisp and flawlessly groomed as you might expect. To qualify, simply switch to our high interest account using our hassle-free switching service.

The struggle ahead will be fierce

It took us only a moment to conclude that this was indeed the route by which the others had descended. When did you last go shopping for clouds? Drapery is the most tangible expression of representational realism yet fishing with rod and line from a herring drifter can also be a most rewarding experience. How do you teach somebody to improvise? The weather closed in overnight, hiding the mountains behind a coating of thick, grey cloud. In a totally sane society, madness is the only freedom. Although the men did most of the talking, it was obvious from the outset that the women were in charge. If you are making a selection of salads at home, always start with a variety of basic ingredients.

It was like stepping into the abyss

Resistance to antibiotics emerges with all bacteria over time yet their questions were pointed, clear and curt. Rarely has such a conclusive result been more necessary. This once passive regime of sun and sand has given away to a more militant mood. The musical vogue at this time was all lilting beats and relaxing vibes yet bees are intelligent and endearing creatures. What about the clouds you never see? For as long as there have been ships there have been wrecks yet there are two major obstacles to any further agreement. The more we learn the more we are fascinated by the complex world of clouds. Out at sea the swell is deeper. Finally, and most obviously, it always pays to study each and every cloud!

The language of clouds

She was a number-cruncher and a creative genius, two factors that didn't do much to bring them together. Yet those of us who are not scientists may have a different response. We can't even predict the next drip from a dripping tap when it becomes irregular. "He's certainly got a nice complexion but he could do with a history lesson". Next year's colours will include fashionable nude, black, sky blue and orchid pink with flashes of neon yellow. Tomorrow, the real debate begins. "Thank god they're wearing different colour ties." He inspected them with some care and eventually allowed himself to be photographed with a cod. Finally, I began to learn the art of angling.

Your proposal may have merit

"Would you like a Knickerbocker Glory?" It's only in the last few days that the worms in my compost heap have become active. There are many species waiting in the wings yet maintaining your figure is a marathon effort, not a sprint. "Will you throw caution to the wind?" "Yes, but we're not going to concentrate on politics, we're going to concentrate on fish." Consumption is usually based on utility or subscription basis with little up-front cost. Lightly season the cod with salt and pepper and heat a little oil in a large non-stick pan. If you succeed it will be a breakthrough in a twenty year campaign. To serve, carefully take the cod from the pan with a fish slice and spoon the clams and butter over the top. There may be side-effects and these may be harmful.

Chinese gold consumption may double

Bracing herself against the eager morning sunlight
she eased the blinds apart. Should we not look for
the first traces of imaginative activity as early as in
childhood? There were chantings and repetitions and
thunderous declamations in uncanny rhythms. They
come closer to the shore after dark and are often
taken from beaches in very shallow water. Nobody
is sure what causes this particular cloud formation
yet a dreamy love song is playing in the background.
Other inconsistencies point in the same direction.
You should give the cockles a final rinse and put them
into a large pan with the white wine. "Off we go again,
ever onwards." Bracing herself against the eager
morning sunlight she eased the blinds apart.

Tomorrow, the real debate begins

His monotone delivery may leave something to be desired yet it offered us an alternative way of looking at the world. "To me, the most important thing is fairness." What we found was a more sophisticated and refined mechanism for how decisions are actually made. Hook sizes can be large as codling have big mouths. Outside the capital, housing experts report that properties are taking an average of eight weeks to sell. "It was shockingly, shudderingly, screamingly cold yet this was better than any swimming pool I'd ever been in." Having learned the ropes, she then graduated to the lifeboat. Worldwide, fish stocks are falling, yet signs of improvement in North Sea cod numbers is encouraging. We are now in a critical and final phase. When is a decision likely to be made?

Fear, anxiety and indecision

Is John Adams America's greatest living composer? All of these techniques involve considerable uncertainty because they haven't been tested under these conditions before. Critics say the estimate is based on an inappropriate scientific technique yet for all its lack of grace, the cod is not an unlovely fish. "I love the idea of doing something that is purely creative, weird and wonderful," she said. It was the golden age of advertising and we felt we owned the world. Thanks to conservation efforts the North Sea Cod is thriving again. This was a provocation ordered from the outside yet they went so far as to evacuate the entire population of the island. Venetians are not exactly boastful, just convinced of their superiority. If you turn to the music this description seems less apt yet storm clouds are gathering and the crisis is imminent.

Is this a kangaroo court?

Little has been done to improve the record of business transparency yet I'm all in favour of the use of sporting tackle. There is so much emphasis on socialising and networking that the work often goes undone. Fashion should be joyful and adventurous but it's also good to be surrounded by like-minded people. These days it's clear that the text is being eased out by the image. A few decades ago cod was a cheap and plentiful source of food yet his previous employers were wrong in having credited him with having no imagination. There's a serious risk of rioting in the streets. Do you feel comfortable talking about this now or do you have to be careful what you say? He missed the sound of breathing and the rustling of clothes yet somewhere along the way you have to pick up practical experience.

The voices of doubt

I have encountered many strange foods on my
journey around the globe yet it is my intention
to ensure that *this* product is known at an international
level. It takes around sixty working hours to make
a suit. For après-ski there is a large bar with sports
tv, restaurant, bowling alley, pool table and arcade.
Failure to address the issue directly could prevent
lessons being learned yet the state of the global
economy is more precarious than recent data suggests.
Scientists have discovered that pigeon flocks are
governed by a kind of democratic hierarchy. In the
long run, the resolution of this struggle may prove
to be political rather than economic yet lot of people
around here are still surviving on a dollar a day.

Health and safety

Everything has to be looked at afresh, with a sniper's eye for detail. What is unreasonable is the sheer scale of cuts facing this sector yet his fame and reputation are now so great that everything he makes can be sold for a fortune. Handsome canopies and intricate ironworks are still part of the scene. Rescue teams will have to work quickly as the rate of the spill could be four or five times the official figure. You could think of it as the cinematic equivalent of window shopping yet research also suggests there is a class divide in the consumption of fast food. Just because they are scavengers doesn't mean they are to be pitied. In the past I've been somewhat squeamish about eating fish yet a little rubbing rendered the deeply-cut inscriptions quite legible. It was damp in the cottage, damp, chill and oppressive.

More snow is on the way

There were literally thousands of these creatures and
I remember thinking at the time that they could not be
very nourishing. As any good teacher knows, education
is only partly about delivering information. From the
wreckers point of view they were doing no more than
reclaiming what was rightfully theirs. In addition, they felt
they needed to improve their ability to handle complexity
and ambiguity. He was looking for a way out of modern
civilization yet the opposite of play is not what is serious
but what is real. The common toad may be ugly, warty
and squat but it is blessed with an extraordinary gift. Your
bait must be in the right spot if you are going to catch them
in numbers. In the sudden silence there is nothing except
the slurp of the swell against the hull but the pirates have
captured the stockade and taken Jim Hawkins hostage.

The word cloud

Like the gannet, the puffin spends the majority of its life on the high seas yet the last thing she wanted to do was build an empire. Tonight there will be drizzle in the far south west. As the bids for the Kandinskys and the Legers came in, she sat on a podium, surveying the elegant assembly below. It's never been a better time to be an eco-builder yet the cash value of gold is trivial compared to its symbolic importance. Of course, none of this will matter if she doesn't get her head straight and perform. Clouds of a more sedate variety are associated with cold ocean currents yet this crisis still has a long way to run. Are you a painter in the Cubist idiom? This mere metal has meaning far beyond price tags but I really don't want another half century of wasted dreams. Luckily, I still had my wits about me.

The empire builder

"I thought the system would eventually correct itself but in fact it's got a lot worse." Picasso is the world's most stolen artist. Luckily I still had my wits about me as a third suspicious letter was in an unknown tongue and even an unknown alphabet. Are we in for a double-dip recession? She is very precise about the possible benefits but not about the dangers, yet he knew more of hooliganism than anarchism. She is photographed on stage in a blue tank-top and red shorts. In the photograph on my right all the detail has been completely altered yet anybody who thinks he can predict the consequences should not be trusted. We have fully equipped, dedicated fashion studios, where you will be able to access a variety of industrial machinery. Luckily, I still have my wits about me.

Wild beasts

Did you know that trombonists are among a select
group of professionals who are allowed to retire early?
If the thief doesn't get rid of these paintings quickly
he will be left with an albatross of enormous proportions
around his neck. Do I detect a trace of déjà vu? After an
hour most of the crowd melted away and the security
forces disappeared shortly after. You will cover all aspects
of the industry and be fully submerged in the design
profession from start to finish. Then there was the matter
of the sounds beneath the earth. We are amid the ruins of
a city after the quake yet the detail remains sketchy. Their
paintings, full of distortion and flat patterns, and painted
in violent colour, created a furore. Shall we go fishing
for dark secrets?

That's the way to do it

Distance learning is the most flexible form of study and is ideal if your job involves travel or irregular working hours. The painting had suffered no damage but a first glance confirmed that a skilled hand had been at work. This is heavy oil we are seeing yet the chances of success are less than fifty/fifty. Are we all living with our heads in the clouds? In mass society, ways of thinking become as standardized as ways of dressing, yet there is also the issue of ethical constraints on research. Are you a climate-change sceptic? Political solutions deserve another shot before we throw in the towel and settle for corporate codes and the privatisation of collective rights. Following me clumsily to her study she asked me for some whiskey to steady her nerves. Hideous and unsettlingly alien, it swam into the blackness and disappeared.

The girl with the pirate tattoo

To view these documents you might need to load some software. It's beneath the waves that most of the action is taking place yet we are speaking these words into the darkness. An early front-runner for thriller of the year, this is tense, intelligent stuff with a meaty run-time and little in the way of flashy quick fixes. Documents are often created to hide, rather than reveal, crucial data, yet the classification of clouds is surely a nebulous pursuit. Please note this position is subject to a standard Criminal Record Bureau check and is not suitable for jobshare.
"As a model you wear what's given to you but this whole deportment thing is a bit uptight for me. I'd rather do yoga or pilates." Curators say there will be a good mix of genres as well as strong representation from international artists.

In search of big fish

She was a complex and slippery character but she was living in a complex and slippery world. Forecasters predict above average temperatures yet it would be wrong to pretend that this stretch of the country has suddenly turned radical. Just like seabirds, pirates are much more at home at sea than on land. "What wouldn't I give for a very powerful torch." You can work out for as little or as long as you want yet clouds are the wild cards in climate change prediction. Meet the sand eel, the unsung hero of the undersea world. What sort of advice are we giving passengers? Yet volcanic ash is still causing travel restrictions and delay. Thirteen reported stress-related health problems, including shingles, psoriasis and panic attacks. The exhibition may finish with a racy Egon Schiele, called *Two Women Embracing*. Since you are a journalist, this is off the record!

Without sponsors there is no expedition

As the economic cycle has swung from boom to bust, punk presents itself as a spirited response to the crisis. Somehow, in the dark, it's easier to remember what you want to be. An independent commission will examine ways to break up the banks but it's the diaries that will attract most interest. Where there are fish to catch, these guys don't mess around, yet this is a vast area of sea and so far we've drawn a blank. Simple, unornamented clothes are set to storm the high street this summer. He had some claim to have painted the first abstract picture but I must say I'm a bit disturbed by all that domestic violence. Are we still having talks about talks? They (mullet) are no lovers of wind or ruffled water and will sink into the deep under these conditions.

Living in the past

"I didn't see a thing. I had my hands over my eyes." Somehow, she made it sound like a compliment yet cloud computing customers don't generally own the means of production. All artists are showmen! When the whales finally did appear it was in spectacular fashion. Even fools will speak wisely in my new language for they will lack the materials to do otherwise. Please sir, can you give me a job? We are starting to see celebrity fashion which the average person on the street can replicate. Tens of thousands have died and many more have been driven from their homes. It's our money and we have a right to know what's happened to it. This is a mandatory appointment and if you do not attend your benefit could be affected.

The gathering storm

Swallows prefer open country and are much less common than swifts in our urban areas. Perhaps, at the end of the day, a degree of anonymity is a wonderful thing. Quicksands are another danger but usually their location is well-known locally. Birds which feed far out to sea are dependent on healthy fish stocks yet even a misfit with no discernable ability can conquer the world. There's something about the smell of suntan lotion. Throughout the day I had the feeling that my luck was beginning to change but in many ways the music was immaterial. Has highly-educated thuggery always gone on and been hushed up? They seem like a truly enlightened party, the only one which understands young people. In addition, they are water-repellent, machine-washable and quick-drying. You don't want to be surrounded by an entourage simply for your own protection yet in the end it was a question of style over substance.

The gravy train

It's all about questioning social and political
attitudes and changing them to really push
the boundaries of design. House martins can
be seen in towns, villages and open terrain.
American forces leave behind a country which
is barely a floating wreck. Yet his sky is always
filled with clouds and places like this represent
a healthy future for us all. Safety is a priority
and we take this very seriously. Against this bleak
outlook, swifts may bring relief. The key fashion
item for next season is a sheepskin aviator jacket
yet safety is a priority and we take this very
seriously. It's a good job Odysseus didn't leave
a carbon footprint.

The American Dream

Outside in the garden he could still hear the peacocks screaming. If you only buy one thing this year it had better be sheepskin. This strike is a political strike, make no mistake, yet the bed is unused and the sheets are cold. What we are looking at today are the pleasures that have gone on throughout the centuries. Most of the complaints came from the liberal fringe yet the history of the world is full of similar examples. How does volcanic ash impact on aircraft performance? If the paintings are not found quickly it could take decades for them to be recovered. O time, thou must untangle this, not I, it is too hard a knot for me to untie. This indeed proved the beginning of a new policy of secrecy yet the public are overwhelmingly against the renewing of Trident.

Morning glory

We are calling for a truly sustainable solution with a minimal environmental impact. Cautionary tales emerge from a different mindset yet her writing is as serious and acute as it is unsentimental. Small ponds and open wildlife areas will be encouraged in our new information pack yet there is growing concern that the wetland environment is suffering from a loss of beaver activity. She is fun to talk with and has a balanced but slightly risqué sense of humour. Is it the textbooks that make maths so dull and tedious? I said nothing and when he resumed speaking his voice was closer to normal. Packed like pilchards, fishermen come here for strong tea, Guinness stew and to catch up with the fishing news.

How to spot a swallow

Some areas will erode while others may silt up entirely yet each time a butterfly is seen its exact location is recorded. You *will* participate in a wide range of external projects and educational trips. For more information about our charges and rates please consult our online price list. To put it simply Sid had no aptitude for playing the bass yet I don't listen to radio anymore because I have a tv. Designer knock-offs, once a novelty, have become common and no longer satisfy fashion-literate consumers. It's a polemic and a dazzlingly argued one at that. Puffins nest underground in old rabbit tunnels but even with local help they are incredibly hard to find.

Their lofty aims

After a long journey why not relax a little. I can't say it was a happy environment to be working in but just how corrosive is the influence of money? You should certainly follow any instructions regarding dosage very carefully. Are our notions of individual continuity simply an illusion? While the speed of communication has slowed everything down it should be apparent that people are much happier when dipping into a range of subjects. Are you encouraged to think outside of the box? To understand why decisions are made you have to look at how events unfold. Let's get celestial! "You're looking at me so attentively but I don't think you're listening to a word I'm saying." Meanwhile, the prospect of widespread social unrest is growing.

The surveillance state

Are you aware of the debate around iconoclasm?
To do well in robotics you need to be a jack of
all trades but you don't want to stick your hand
into a cow's derriere if you aren't totally sure what
you are doing! Avoid cycling or excessive exercise
for several hours. Surface slicks may account for
as little as 2% of the oil now spilling into the Gulf
of Mexico yet it doesn't take long before you start
cutting into front-line delivery. It is always best to
have heard some of the headlines before getting into
work. He befriended winos and derelicts, sharing
out his cash and belongings, yet they sensed, once
again, that they would find themselves isolated in
splendid heroism.

Meltdown

Whether it was actual bravery that kept him there or extraordinary arrogance is open to some debate. "Ask Nigel how 'industrious' sounds," she said. It's all very vigorous and virile yet this thin-lipped variety has sturdier jaws and more teeth. What are the roots of altruism? "We'll end with a pepper but we're going to begin with porn." He emerges here as a global softie with no time for oppression and all the time in the world for the oppressed. Lavish eating and drinking was a key element of the Roman world yet even now the city seems incapable of self-regulation. This causes an intense acoustic ripple to propagate across the plane of the surface.

Transgression and taboo

It is still not clear what caused the crash yet the focus is now on national security. Once stored in a vacuum these bubbles release spectacular amounts of energy and it is not unusual to experience swelling or discomfort for a few days after the operation. Although we don't yet know why singing should help it has been suggested that music can be an aid to memory. Yes, but are these paintings here to advertise a licentious lifestyle? Fierce debates still rage about these campaigns yet we are as a nation uniquely diffident. It has often been said that periods of serious instability produce great art, in which case we are surely in for a new Renaissance. We should archive as much of this material as possible before it disappears. A self-deprecating charm is often an authentic trait; talking of which, you might like to discover the beneficial qualities of clouds. Everything that is solid melts into air.

www.ingramcontent.com/pod-product-compliance
Ingram Content Group UK Ltd.
Pitfield, Milton Keynes, MK11 3LW, UK
UKHW042004230426
12048UKWH00009B/536